Darlene

FICTION WRITING
How to Write Your First Novel

~~∽∾~~

Karleene Morrow

I look forward to reading your first novel. Write on.

Karleene Morrow

Published by
Agate Beach Press, PO Box 864, Newport OR 97365

Manufactured in the United States of America

ISBN 1480298859

© Cover design Charlie Magee, Signal Design Inc.,
Eugene Oregon

Website: http://www.karleenemorrow.com/

🐾 ~~~Table of Contents~~~ 🐾

▲~~Author's Note~~▼

Let me say right off, fiction writing is a craft. It can be learned. Contrary to popular belief writing is not a talent, although someone who brings talent to the table has a head start on becoming a good writer, quite possibly a great one. Dedicate yourself to learning the techniques of this craft and you can write fiction. It is almost a given that if a person does that, and writes consistently, creative juices will begin to flow that he didn't know he possessed.

This book is not all-inclusive and there is much about the craft of writing that it does not detail. But there is no fluff in it. It is packed with the nitty-gritty. The pages are full of tips and techniques and will also guide you to further information and study. Hopefully it will be of considerable help as you begin your writing journey.

❧⌘⌘❧

ᔠᔠᔠ~~~DEDICATION~~~ᔦᔦᔦ

Mariah Matthews

For all the writing skills you taught me,

And all the writing skills we learned together

ᔦᥴᔡᔰᔡᔦ

◁~~A NOTE OF APPRECIATION~~▷

I am grateful once again for the critiques and advice from fellow writers of the Oregon Coast Writers Focus Group: Mariah Matthews, Sunshine Keck, M.C. (Marge) Arvanitis, Patsy Brookshire and Kelli Brugh. Somehow these women manage to catch not only the big goofs but also the smallest detail as they listen to chapters of whatever I'm reading at the time. Lately it has been this book of fiction tips. If it has turned out to be as good as I hope, I have to thank them for having "a good ear" and for their willingness to spend whatever time was needed to get each section right.

Special thanks to Sunshine Keck, our Focus Copy Editor Extraordinaire.

Every writer should be so fortunate in finding a caring critique group that is not a critical group. There is a measurable – and emotional – difference between the two. Thank you writer-friends. When I count my blessings you are all high on the list.

⋘⋙

FICTION WRITING
How to Write Your First Novel

Karleene Morrow

❧~~~One~~~☙

The Secret to Starting Your First Novel

I wish I'd had a little book like this when I wrote my first novel. I decided to write this one to help others who find themselves in the same situation. You probably have the germ of an idea for your story. Perhaps you've written several sentences or several paragraphs or twenty pages. Maybe you have spent a considerable amount of time outlining, or creating scenarios over forty-eight chapters.

Whatever you have noted as the story you want to tell, now is the time to begin telling it. You've dragged your feet because you're not sure where to start. I'm going to share with you the secret of starting your first novel. Actually, it is the secret to writing the entire novel. Here it is:

Write.

Then write some more.

Then write more after that.

And then keep on writing.

You can think and plan and ruminate all you want, but if you want to write, at some point you are going to have to plant your backside in a chair and pick up a pen or put your fingers on a keyboard.

Where to start? Here's another dirty little secret—nobody knows where to start. Every story is different. Start at the beginning, or what you think is the beginning. By the time you learn the Elements of writing (reading in the evenings) and the Techniques of writing (studying in the mornings) you will already have discovered a good deal about your story. It likely will change. It surely will grow. It might be that the beginning will need to be tossed out, at which point you'll experience the pain and agony of killing your darlings. But you're apt to find, as have so many writers before you, that the book is considerably better if the first few chapters are tossed and then the story starts. Maybe that's where it needed to start, the first chapters being just warm-ups, and the reader didn't need all that getting-ready-stuff. If you have to toss it and there was important material there, you'll find the best places to work those scenes into later chapters of the book, maybe as flashbacks or backstory.

Many writers sweat through a complete novel, or two or three, before they hit their stride and produce quality, or at least publishable, work. Some though, nail that first novel and you may be one of them. It is a given, however, that the first draft of that book may be a sad state of writing. Anne R. Allen in her co-authored book, *How To Be a Writer in the E-Age,* calls it the "sucky first draft." If you can't recognize its quality or non-quality, put it away for three or four weeks without touching it. When you go back to it, to the very beginning, you're going to see it for what it is. Start your second draft, or what is called, the rewrite. Be prepared - it might not be your only rewrite.

You may be comforted to know how the literary icon and Pulitzer Prize winner James A. Michener (1907-1997,) wrote his first drafts. He did some by hand and some on an old key banger Underwood typewriter. He wrote one sentence after another until he reached the end of a chapter. Then he started the next chapter. He did not self-edit, correct, or go back to search facts or 'fix' in any way. He went from start to finish. I saw a copy of the first draft rewrite of one of his manuscripts. He started on page one with pencil in hand and began the changes, cross-outs, mark-ups, margin notes, arrows and inserted words until the pages were completely unreadable by anyone except him. It was indeed a sucky first draft, and in his opinion all his firsts were just that. Then he began typing the second draft. By the time he reached his final rewrite, the polished story was far beyond and better than that first draft. Michener always said he wasn't much of a writer but he was a great re-writer.

If you have read or even seen one of Michener's awesome thousand-page tomes it should scramble your mind to even think about this undertaking. The prolific master did not use a computer. In his later works computers were certainly available but he eschewed the use of one. He did, finally, capitulate to an Olympic electric typewriter. He wrote more than forty titles, which sold somewhere beyond seventy-five million copies and continue to sell today.

The point is that Michener did not stop once he began writing. What is the importance of this? Once the juices begin flowing and the story begins telling itself, to stop and 'go back' for whatever reason is an interruption the writer does not need, according to Michener. Interestingly, it is the belief and the system that many authors use today.

We'll be talking quite a bit about the techniques of writing. You'll want to also learn techniques from other sources, books, writing tips online or your Wednesday evening community college writing class. If you are able to find a good critique group to join it will become your most valuable tool. Be cautious of those groups who like to criticize, which is not the same as helpful critiquing. Bail out of those types quickly. A good critique group offers respectful, constructive suggestions but defers to the author for any changes.

Now it is time to start writing. Set up your writing place, the private area you will go to each and every day at the same time. It can be as elaborate as you want or need it to be or a cubbyhole closet. The important thing is that it is your private space. And let me repeat, you will go there every day at the same time. Do not allow intrusions such as family requests, telephone calls or anything else to interfere with your writing time. Plan ahead and schedule the time that is going to be yours. Let's say 9 a.m. is your writing time or 6 a.m. or 9 p.m. You set the time that you can live with. Advise your family ahead of time. Go to your private place at your planned time. Every day.

Next, set the number of words you are going to complete at each session, maybe five hundred or two thousand, whatever is a workable goal for you. Start writing and keep on writing, even if two paragraphs later you realize you could have said it better. Don't be tempted to go back. Go forward. Do not give yourself permission to leave the task until you have completed your daily goal. When you do finish, you will probably find that you also need to set up pages for characters. You might already be getting confused about what color that certain character's hair was. It is an excellent plan to list your characters and then write down everything you know, or ultimately discover, about them. The reader will not need to know every specific thing about the character, but you do.

Do not fool yourself by setting the duration of time you will spend at your writing station. You will learn fairly rapidly that if you set three hours, you'll get very proficient at wasting three hours. It will be gone and very likely will not have your desired number of words.

Before we finish with this discussion of how to "start" let me tell you of a software program that might make your life considerably easier as a fiction writer. Some writers like to use software writing programs and some hate them. If you want to try one, yWriter5 is a free program. Google it and you will see the latest versions and be able to go to the URL.

It is written for Windows. Once you install it, there is a Quick Start Guide and also a user's manual. You can use this or any program you might like better, to organize your story, characters, settings and equally important, to write your novel. It is designed for novel formatting whereas Word is not. However, when you are finished your work can be converted to Word for submissions. Scrivener's is a high quality program with versions available for both Mac and Windows. It is not free, however. I like MSWord and have not yet written a book using writing software, so cannot comment intelligently on its value.

One last little prod. If you want to write fiction, you also need to read fiction. Most books on writing will urge you to do this. More on the subject later.

Write on.

♠~~~Two~~~♥

"How to" For New Writers

Must a newcomer learn every minute detail of the writing craft—the components, rules, shapes and nuances that make one book work and the next fail—before he can take up a pen or sit down to the computer? It is true that a person should bring to the table a foundation in English composition. You will be better off in the long haul if you or someone else does not have to edit a grammar or spelling mess on your first rewrite. You'll need to understand more than a grasp of grammar to be a writer, a writer who anyone wants to read, but that will suffice as you get started.

As to the rules of writing, the fact is that most writers just start writing, then learn the how's and why's as they go along. That might even be the best way, since when you are studying some part of the craft, dialogue, for example, you will have written dialogue and will be more able to relate the lessons to your own attempts. Author

James Scott Bell says that he has shelves full of books on writing. He wrote, "I've read every one with a yellow highlighter. Then I've read almost all of them with a red, felt-tip pen, marking things I missed the first time." He even went through some of them a third time, writing out new insights on a yellow legal pad.

Even if you start writing now, tonight, do buy a good book on writing and read it, absorb it, understand it. When you finish it, buy another one. There are some duds out there but there are also many good ones, just a few of which are:

Plot & Structure, by James Scott Bell
Stein on Writing, by Sol Stein
On Writing, by Stephen King
The Elements of Style, by Strunk & White

Stephen King's book is amazing and *The Elements of Style* is critical. Both of these should be in every writer's library,

Perhaps you don't know your story yet but you have an idea. Good. Write it down even if you only have a sentence of two. Maybe something like this:

Jeremy wants to have one last fling with his best friend, Tom, before he gets married. He and Tom fly to Paris for a week vacation and on the second night Jeremy mysteriously disappears.

You want it to be a paranormal? All right. The boys' parents have given them trips as graduation presents. They fly to Paris, spending the second night in a loud bar that is rocking with music and foxy French girls who like to dance. When the bar closes they step outside and are attacked. It's dark, they can't see their attackers clearly but they seem more animal than human. Jeremy is bitten.

You'd prefer time travel? This then: Same scenario, but when the boys step out of the bar Paris is not as it was. The streets are cobbled and dark, gas lamps pierce the fog with only a blister of light. They're forced to leap back as a large black coach and four roar out of the fog, clattering and rattling past them. The man in the box has a whip in his raised fist.

Whatever your idea, put down your sentence or paragraph or as much as you know about the story you want to write. If you have some ideas of events you want to happen during the story, write those down. As you progress add whatever other thoughts may come to you, even if they seem silly or unrelated. First thoughts are often best thoughts and they may take you somewhere you didn't expect to go when you come back to view them later. It doesn't matter if you don't know how you want the book to end. Write—the ending will come to you in plenty of time, maybe several endings from which you'll have to chose. You're not building your masterpiece now, you're putting down your ideas, so don't spend excess time on style or grammar or run-on sentences. You get to do that soon enough. Just put your fingers onto your keyboard or grip your pen, whatever feels best to get these ideas out of your head and onto paper or into a word processing file.

There are those who prefer to work from a skeleton of not much more than you just wrote. That is too sparse for some people. There are writers who must know every chapter, outlined and in detail before they sit down to fill in and flesh out. There are also those who can't abide outlining. One person said it felt like a term paper. Stephen King wouldn't consider it, as you'll discover when you read him. Writers approach their work in different ways but I'd be willing to say that every last one of them has encountered surprises. Planned scenes change. Unplanned scenes appear out of virtually nowhere. A character not in the skeletal outline comes along and just muscles his way in. Then another one appears and he wants to take over the story, while you, the author, can barley make him shut up.

Your Muse will appear when you are least expecting him (or her.) The Muse can't be summoned but does eventually come to almost every if not all writers. New writers don't believe this when they first hear it but it happens again and again. Even a seasoned, veteran author experiences those types of intrusions that mostly turn out well with new scenes or characters demanding stage time.

I have a quote taped to the top of my monitor that says:

The Muse proves more and more elusive the longer
you await it,
but it is remarkably available if you go to seek it
every day
and grab it by the throat.

I don't know the author of that insightful statement,
but it seems to me his last name might be Boccia. If
someone knows, I would be grateful to be apprised of
same.

Write your ideas for the story. Get as much down as
you can and then we'll see if we can take this to the next
level.

✱~~~Three~~~✱

So What About Those Prologues?

As we've discussed, our writing goal as we begin our novels is to Hook the Reader. Thus: to prologue or not to prologue, that is the question. And if you ask enough writing teachers and other writers or read books on writing, you'll more than likely get a plethora of advice. And half of it will say, No, No prologues, agents hate them.

Really?

I have no proof to contest that except I would ask, why is it that we have read and continue to read prologues? I'm an avid reader. I read every night for a few to several hours. I have read multitudes of books – and I see many prologues. Example? I recently finished *The Kitchen House* – yes, prologue. Before that, *Water For Elephants* – yes, prologue. How about James Patterson's *Blink?* Yes, prologue. Octavia Butler's

Kindred? S.J.Bolton's *Sacrifice*? Meltzer's *The Inner Circle?* Yes, prologues all.

But *Murder in the Marias*, *The Help*, any of Michael Connelly's books? No, no prologues. And Lawrence Block? Not a chance. I can't imagine Block using prologues, but maybe he has and I'll have to eat humble pie since admittedly I haven't read *everything* he's written. But I am rather seriously committed to his Matt Scudder books. No prologues.

The point is, using prologues seems to be at the writer' discretion. If agents hate them it certainly isn't preventing them from shopping the books they like to their publishers. When, then, would a prologue be appropriate or useful?

Some writers use the prologue for an introduction that is shocking, or frightening, or maybe someone dies or is murdered but the reader is not told who the victim is. These types of prologues are usually scenes without sequels and are used to hook the reader. They don't even have to include the protagonist but it's a good idea if they at least relate to the story about to be told.

Often a writer, usually a new writer, wants to set the stage, give the background of the story or the character so 'the reader can relate.' This, according to comments by publishers and agents when discussing their slush piles, generally gets out of hand and results in a long-winded, boring epistle that would not only turn a reader off but she probably would not have purchased the book in the first place if that is what greeted her as she thumbed it in a bookstore. Or she read the online sample offered for an e-book.

Information about the character, if it's pertinent, should be woven into the story itself by use of dialogue or flashback. Any backstory the writer wants or needs to put up front as a prologue should be relatively brief, a few pages. A good example of this type of prologue was used all the way back to Victorian fiction. Willie Collins, a friend of Charles Dickens, uses a short prologue to give the Indian background in his detective novel, The Moonstone.

Many books, frequently murder/crime genres, set up something in the prologue that grabs the readers, but is not mentioned again until later in the book. Or in some cases, the end of the book is a repeat of the beginning but it has a conclusion that in some way satisfies the questions raised at the start. It is a challenge to write beginnings and endings in this manner, but in the hands of an accomplished writer it has been done and will continue to be. In the older movie, No Way Out. (still shown now and then on TV) Kevin Costner is stamping around a room with two thugs watching him, ranting about some unknown person who won't come out from behind a closed door. Then words come on the screen: Six Months Earlier. The story begins and works its way forward until it comes to a startling conclusion in the same room when the unknown person opens the door and steps out. Similar styles of the prologue have been used in many novels and movies.

Whichever type of prologue or whatever reason for using one, it must engage the reader, make her want to read more. If it doesn't, rewrite or throw it out. When you feel you have the prologue just right, ignore it for a few weeks. Don't re-read it during that time. And don't bother asking your friends or even casual acquaintances about the opening. They do not want to hurt your feelings and will generally either praise it or say something vague. In either case you are not likely to get real help from them. Go back later then and do your best to read it as if you were a book browser, deciding whether or not to buy. Consider its merits and if you belong to a critique or writer's group, this is the time to take it to them, read it aloud and be open to any advice they have. Then remind yourself that this is the first draft you'll be rewriting one or more times.

Beginnings often change by the time we reach the end of our novels. You'll most likely rewrite that prologue, or the first chapter, a time or two. Remind yourself that it is your beginning. It is one of the most important parts of your entire book because if it doesn't capture the potential buyer, the rest of the book, no matter how excellent, will be ignored as your buyer moves on. Keep your goal in mind: hook the reader.

ഇ~~~Four~~~ഇ

How to Keep Readers Turning Pages

All right new writers, you've set up your writing area, you go there every day and churn out x number of words on the story you have set out to tell. Kudos. But along with writing your dream, there are techniques you need to know, techniques that make a story sizzle and lack of which will leave a story falling flat. Among these are developing characters, components of the story, that is, beginnings, middles and endings, building plot, dialogue, diction, style, scene and sequel, point of view, tight writing. . . and more.

Along with writing every day, it helps to also learn something about the craft every day. Each strategy a writer learns will benefit him as a writer. It is important, one could say imperative, to work at learning the craft of writing on a continual basis and not think that the book should be written first, then the skills learned and the book 'fixed' afterward. Wrong approach. The more one learns the more improved the writing process and certainly the better the manuscript that is coming into being. Lack of writing basics is undoubtedly the prime reason that many first novels end up in the bottom drawer and subsequent novels see print. The more we learn and the more we write, using that combination together, the finer writers we are going to be.

That is not to say we should sweat over each word or phrase in our first draft. On the contrary, my belief, influenced by wiser writers such as James Michener and Stephen King, is that it is to our benefit to write 'straight through.' Write the first draft without looking back. By the end of it you will have an understanding of the story that was not available to you when you began. The rewrites, however many it takes, will bring the novel out in all of its potential. But the more we know about the art and craft of story telling, the better both the first draft and subsequent rewrites are going to be.

It is difficult, or maybe impossible, to say that one technique is more important than another. Interesting characters, for example, will not save a novel that is loosely written and perhaps abounds with exposition, page after page of description. Yawn.

There are, however, two parts of the writing process that rise to the top in importance. The first is keeping your novel "active" right out of the chute. That means show, not tell. You will hear that over and over if you work at learning the craft of writing. As you read and study you will continually be told to write in the active voice or to not write in the passive voice. Listen up. The passive voice will kill your story, it will make it drag, be boring and will lose all but the most masochistic of readers. Seriously. It is self-torture to try to stay with a dragging, boring story unless there is nothing else in the house to read except the toothpaste carton.

Showing is letting the reader see the scene or event. *Telling* is having the reader hear the event. It is explaining. Sometimes telling works but basically it is lazy writing. "The morning was bright and warm." What's wrong with that sentence? Not much. The grammar is correct, it has a subject and a verb. But it is passive. The sentence is telling us something. It is explaining. What about: The day dawned bright and warm. Ahh, now we see it, we feel it rather than hearing it. "My front window was broken by your son." Passive. "Your son broke my front window." Active. Better.

If a character is mean and abusive, don't tell us that. Show us something in his actions, allow us to experience him. When we see a character in his actions we invest our emotions. If we only hear about him he becomes the same kind of fact that we read in a newspaper or hear about on the news.

What would you think of this: "It was the last morning of Virginia's bloodiest year since the Civil War. There was a fire burning and through the window sunrise would show the sea." Sound all right?

Or maybe this instead: "On the last morning of Virginia's bloodiest year since the Civil War, I built a fire and sat facing a window of darkness where at sunrise I knew I would find the sea." Does that sound, feel, read better? Yes, I'd say so. That's the opening to Patricia Cornwell's Cause of Death. Excellent writing.

While you're focusing on the active voice, there's something related that you should be aware of. Please do not have a character tell another character something she already knows. Do not have Jane say "I ran into your friend Betty, the hair dresser, today." She knows her friend is a hairdresser. That's sloppy writing, used when the author butts in to *tell* the reader something he should have *shown*. Learn all you can about showing and not telling. Use the active voice. It will be one of the two biggest favors you do yourself as an emerging writer.

One way you can help yourself stay on track is to use the Search feature on your word processing program when you finish a chapter. Look for "was." Most of the time you will see a passive sentence. Rewrite it. Make the 'was' search a routine until you are absolutely certain that you have overcome the habit of writing in the passive voice. Also turn on your grammar and spelling feature and watch for those green underlines. The program, not being human, is often wrong so skip those notices but it's not generally wrong about a passive sentence. Rewrite to make the sentence active and you will see instant improvement.

The subject of show and tell encompasses more than active or passive sentences. In fiction, exposition delivers background information about the plot or characters and their history. It can also turn into a long-winded discourse on the countryside or even the weather. It may become the prologue itself where the reader is told events that happened before the novel starts.

Exposition is like horseradish. The writer will want to use it sparingly. Part of exposition is narrative summary and that technique can be beneficial. For example, consider how to take a story forward, beyond the repetitive days of a beach vacation. Rather than describing each day's events as clones of the day before, the writer may use a short narrative summary and move on to the vacation scenes that are supportive of the plot.

The narrative summary then would come under "telling." The scenes in the book need to be shown in the "now" or in what we call real time. We want our scenes to progress as though they were happening in front of the reader's eyes. Even in flashback scenes, the events need to unfold as if they are happening in real time. Writers must include action to bring scenes to life. That action may be anything from murder to raising a teacup to one's lips.

Exposition and long narratives were popular in earlier fiction but in today's literary world telling does not work well. Lengthy passages tend to feel boring and more like lectures. Readers today may or may not be more sophisticated than those of earlier years, but they certainly prefer faster moving stories.

Show more and tell less. Your novel will have a better chance of success.

The second technique a writer should know if he wants to keep his readers turning pages is to end each chapter with something unresolved, something that makes the readers want to go on. It does not have to be a major event like the house burning down or a burglar crawling through a window. But if the chapter ending leaves something the reader is unsure or curious or concerned about, she'll keep reading. This is the kind of writing that readers mean when they say "I couldn't put it down," or "It kept me up half the night." The reader is anxious to know what comes next.

Read the ending of one of your chapters as if you were a new reader. Does it make you want to turn the page? Do you want to know what happens now? If not, analyze that chapter and consider how to make the ending intriguing. Good story line along with good writing engages the reader but dull chapter ending are dangerous. The reader is apt to close the book and maybe never get back to it again.

At a writers' conference in Austin, Texas several years ago, speaker James Magnasom said a friend told him he had finally figured out why Louis L'Amour's books were so popular. When asked why, the friend said, "At the end of each chapter there's a knock at the door."

Put a sticky note on the left corner of your monitor that says 'Show, Don't Tell." On the right corner stick one up that says "Is there a knock at the door?" Keep those in front of you as you write your novel. Whatever else you learn about this craft, these two techniques will be among the most valuable tools in your bag of writing tricks.

℟ ~~~Five~~~ ℟

The Importance of Novel Beginnings

As you work along writing your novel it is critical that you are also taking some time each day to learn more about the techniques of writing. In an earlier chapter I stressed the importance of your reference library and suggested the four books that should be on every writer's bookshelves: *Plot & Structure* by James Scott Bell, *Stein on Writing* by Sol Stein, *On Writing* by Stephen King and *The Elements of Style* by Strunk & White.

As you study these books and others that you add to your library, and in your Internet research, you will come across references to "Beginnings, Middles and Endings." Novels, like plays, can be dissected into three parts, or three acts. Act one, or the beginning, will surely be the greatest challenge of the three acts although each "Act" will have its own demands.

You may have full knowledge or only a basic rough idea of the plot, the story you want to tell. You've decided on writing in first or third person. You know the genre and tone, such as sci-fi, romance, thriller, epic or other and if your story will be humorous, loopy, serious, fast-paced or slow nerve-wracking suspense. You must bring this much to the table before you are ready to address beginnings, middles and endings.

In the beginning your goal is to:

Hook the Reader

Establish, or hint at, a dramatic situation

Tell us the setting and time

Introduce at least one character

Introduce the opposition

Hooking the reader is a term you will hear repeatedly. Its importance cannot be overstressed. You must make the reader want to read more and you must do it quickly. A reader is not all that different from an agent considering your manuscript. If that first paragraph or two, or to some readers or agents that very first sentence, does not generate interest and make one want to read more, it won't matter if you write a good book because sadly, it won't get read.

Go to your local library or to Amazon or another eSeller if you want to do this online. Spend some time reading the openings of one book after another. Look at the best sellers as well as obscure novels you never heard of. What is it in the openings that make you want to continue reading? I believe that in every successful novel you'll see or feel intrigue; a question has been raised in your mind and you are impelled to read on. You are pulled deeper into the story. You have just been hooked.

Many years ago I read a detective novel, long since forgotten, possibly by Raymond Chandler. I can't quote the opening exactly, but it went something like this: "My partner and I were just finishing our shift and getting ready to head back to the precinct when someone threw the girl off the bridge."

Holy buckets! Is this a book you'd put back on the shelf? I don't think so.

Or what about this one: "Hapscomb's Texaco sat on Number 93 just north of Arnette, a piss-ant four street berg about 110 miles from Houston. Tonight the regulars were there, sitting by the cash register, drinking beer, talking idly, watching the bugs fly into the big lighted sign. It was Bill Hapscomb's station, so the others deferred to him even though he was a pure fool."

Want more? Sure you do and so did ten million others who read Stephen King's *The Stand.*

And what about the famous ones: "Call me Ishmael." *Moby Dick.* Or "I wish I could tell you about the South Pacific. The way it was." *Tales from the South Pacific.*

While all openings won't be as dramatic as these, all good first scenes have this effect on readers. We can't resist. We want to know more. Work on your opening lines until you are convinced that they will grab readers with a firm grip.

Introduce us quickly to a character with whom we can identify, whether or not he is the protagonist. If the author opens the novel with information he thinks we need to know before getting on with the story everything is immediately slowed down. Exposition always slows a story and too much of it turns a story boring. As an opening it basically kills a novel before it even gets breathing. Unless maybe you're Michener. He could write 300 pages about a beaver dam and some Indians before he even started the story itself. If you are not Michener, think "action" as you create those first lines. You can explain later. And of course you'll want to work it into the story, not feed it to the reader in long dull ramblings.

Another beginning to avoid is to open with a dream. Readers don't like it and agents hate it. It is another death knell to your novel so don't be tempted.

Once you have your opening hook you can then start building your plot. Conflict, or opposition to your protagonist's wants or goals, should be introduced early, at least in the first third of the book. The sooner the better even if it is only alluded to, not shown in detail. The details can be worked continually through the story events. The lead character is thwarted. As he comes close to resolving the problem, he is slammed into another obstacle. Continue to build the tension by having him run into one issue after another. At the very least stretch out the resolution to his problem until we as readers are ready to tear out our hair.

Act One, or the first part of your novel, "The Beginning," should have the reader worrying about all of the known or anticipated obstacles that you plan to develop in Act Two, "The Middle" of your book. It is critical to hook the reader but equally important to keep her on the line.

Writing the Middle of Your Novel.

In the previous chapter on Beginnings, we discussed the importance of opening scenes and particularly the first lines in which your goal was to hook the reader. We talked about introducing at least one character early on, possibly two. If you did this, and neither of them are your main character, you have the perfect set up for bringing him onto the stage.

Some novels, some great ones in fact, do not let us meet the main character until late in the first part of the novel, Act One or even the start of Act Two. If you've decided to do that, one way that works well is to have your characters talk about him, praise him, tell interesting stories or raise questions about him. In doing this, by the time we meet him our interest is piqued, we're anxious to know that character.

In the beginning you also put us in the time and place of the story and set up the dramatic situation that will keep us reading over the next few hundred pages. Now as you come to the 'middle' of your book, Act Two as it were, you will be developing the plot. Middles are said to be the most difficult part of the novel writing process, but if you don't buy into that, just work your story, you can get through it with little stress, and actually enjoy doing it. It most likely will be longer than the beginning or the ending. Good. That gives you the broad canvas on which to write the truly important part of the book. The beginning must hook us and the ending must satisfy us. But the middle is the grit of the story itself.

If you've set up conflict as you should have, now is the time to deepen it. You may feel you need to resolve it but don't do that until you've set up the next conflict or obstacle. Once you resolve all the conflicts your story is over even if you didn't intend it to be. Be sure a new conflict overlaps before you resolve the first one. The more obstacles you can believably create, the more tension and the more your reader is going to be turning pages well into the night.

For your story to be a hit, you'll need these obstacles and part or total resolutions for your characters but you'll also need to write good, believable dialog to develop those characters. You want to stay in the point of view you're using. That is not to say you can't change point of view but be careful in doing so. You will confuse readers if you pop around to different points of view. If you are in Bill's POV and he makes a statement but then you write "John didn't argue but he didn't believe that for one minute" you have just switched the viewpoint. The reader can't know what John thinks since we're looking through Bill's eyes. You could write 'John didn't appear to believe that at all.' Now the story has stayed in the same point of view but the reader is given a glimpse of what John might be thinking. Changing points of view is risky. It takes an experienced hand to change POVs in paragraphs. New writers might be wise to limit changes to chapters, making the switch clear perhaps even by giving the chapter a title. Writers learning the craft would be well advised to avoid it. If the Point of View technique is not clear to you, be sure to study it in books or online articles on writing, as this is a point (pun intended) that can seriously squirrel up a story. We will return to POV in a later chapter and discuss it more fully.

Dialogue is another technique the writer should grasp fully. Story characters do not speak the way people speak in real life. If you listen to a nearby conversation when in a restaurant, for example, you'll hear many partial or unfinished sentences, ahs and ums, certainly some bad grammar, abundant adjectives, moralizing, clichés, slang, swearing . . . most of which you do not want in your book. You do, of course, want your characters to speak in a manner than works with who they are. A laid back, easy-going character will not speak the same way that an uptight, stuffed shirt will or a western rancher or a Fargo used car salesman.

Give your story people dialogue that matches who they are, but avoid bogging them or us down in stereotype. If you have started reading a book you decided you hated, go back and look at it. What made you close and set it aside? Maybe the plot line was boring or seemed to be going nowhere, but odds are that dialogue and characters had much to do with your resultant disinterest. In Bell's book *Plot & Structure*, recommended in an earlier chapter, there is good information on dialogue. Also, Gloria Kempton's *Dialogue* from the Write Great Fiction series is considered by many to be a worthwhile treatise of learning to write dialogue. Excellent books on writing are available at major online bookstores and at the Writer's Digest book club. You can purchase books from Writers Digest without belonging to their book club.

Great characters in any story will override a mediocre plot. Not that you should strive for a boring plot but the point is that the characters in your book need to be interesting and believable. If we care about the characters we'll ride along with the plot even if it isn't a truly strong one. Learn all you can about writing characters so you don't write wooden ones. They'll kill a story quickly, even one with an engrossing plot.

While *Lonesome Dove* was an engaging story, the characters were nothing short of memorable. And who can forget Randle McMurphy or Nurse Ratched in *One Flew Over the Cuckoo Nest*? Novels with characters fully developed and alive cannot do anything but succeed. An excellent book on this subject is *Creating Characters,*

How to Build Story People by the acclaimed teacher and writer, Dwight W. Swain.

What exactly is a plot? That question is asked in hundreds of writing classes and everywhere else when a few new writers congregate. It looks like something difficult to grasp, ethereal, elusive, complex. It is none of those. Someone, somewhere, reduced plot to its simplest form. Character + Conflict = Plot. That's about it.

Most books on writing will address plot or at the very least mention it. You'll read various rules of plot, but they'll all crunch down to these as pointed out in *Techniques of Fiction Writing* by Eloise Jarvis McGraw, published in 1959:

1) Who is the character?

2) What does he want?

3) What is preventing him from getting it?

4) What will he do about it?

5) What are the results of his actions?

6) Does he get what he wants or does he get something else?

7) What does the story say?

What the story says is the theme and every story has one. You might have the theme of your novel clear in your mind before you start writing or you may get to the very end before you know what it is as McGraw found - and myself as well. In either case you should be able to state in one sentence what your book says. What is the theme of *Gone with the Wind*? Maybe: We do what we have to do to survive. What about *The Firm*? How about: Money can't buy loyalty or Things aren't always what they seem. *The Hunger Games*? Maybe: Treat others the way you want to be treated.

I don't know what the authors of those books would say their themes are but my guesses might be close. Some writers work with the theme in mind. Some find that to be too restrictive and believe it forces the direction of a story when in fact the characters should be free to develop as they will. (Unless a character steps up and starts to take the story down a path you don't want and you have to rein him in. Believe it, this happens.) Those writers prefer to filter out the theme after the novel is complete. You should do whatever feels right but at some point, know your theme.

Writing teachers address the framework of plot differently but they come down to the same thing. Bell in *Plot & Structure* describes plot with the acronym "LOCK."

L - Lead (Your main character)

O - Objective (Want, Desire)

C - Confrontation (Opposition)

K - Knockout (Resolution, great ending.)

A few other notes to consider:

ADJECTIVES are stronger if used sparingly. We weary after a few paragraphs of overstated description. Be stingy with pumping up your prose with adjectives in an attempt to make it more colorful. Mark Twain's advice was, If you catch an adjective, kill it. Once in awhile though, as pointed out in *The Elements of Style* by Strunk & White, adjectives surprise us with their power:

Up the airy mountain,
Down the rushy glen,

We daren't go a-hunting

For fear of little men. . .

But for the most part, adjectives are only powerful if not overused. If you want to write beautiful, memorable prose, read one of James Lee Burke's books and try to figure out how he does it.

ADVERBS are problematic as well in quality writing. You will sometimes see Mark Twain quoted as saying "If you see an adverb, kill it." He said that about adjectives. What he said about adverbs is "I am dead to *adverbs*; they cannot excite me."

Sad to say, however, you will see many adverbs as tags on speech, including those used by top selling authors (The reason might be that they can get away with it.) It is lazy writing to pen tags like these:

He cried happily

He said gently

He answered miserably

He asked bluntly

A few of those "ly" words go a long way. You'll be a better writer if you work a bit more diligently and write the emotion, not tag with an adverb. You could say: He asked in his blunt way or He said, happiness creasing his face, or some other description of what you want to convey. When you write in a lazy fashion it shows up fast and begins the downward spiral of a reader's interest. In the main, write with nouns and verbs.

As long as we're here, drop those 'He groaned" and other such tags after speech. Occasionally they are usable and suit our purposes. New or inexperienced writers, however, have been known to pack a page of dialogue with them and send a reader screaming.

"What did you do today?" he asked.

"I went shopping in town," she replied.

"What, again?" he complained.

"There were some accessories I needed," she retorted.

"Accessories? Do you think we're made of money?" he barked.

"Now don't start acting like a tightwad again," she demanded.

"Your shopping is going to break the bank around here!" he shouted.

Besides being bad dialogue, the tags are enough to make a reader want to stop reading. We could write the same exchange without the explanation tags and at least improve it.

"What did you do today?" he asked.

"I went shopping in town."

"What again?

She tried to explain to him. "There were some accessories I needed."

"Accessories? Do you think we're made of money?

"Now don't start acting like a tightwad again," she said.

He put his hands on his hips and shouted. "Your shopping is going to break the bank around here."

Notice, too, that in changing the boring rhythm by writing "She tried to explain" and "He put his hands on his hips" the passage was improved. As much as it could be improved.

"He said," is the best tag you can use (and not at the end of every sentence but enough to make it clear who is speaking.) "Said" tends to become invisible; it doesn't pull the reader out of the story.

Be careful, too, with exclamation points. They tend to dominate and make the reader feel he's being shouted at! And never, ever, <u>underline</u>. Both exclamation points and underlining are basically rude, as if the author thinks the reader doesn't get it. Emphasis can be employed occasionally in the right place, but do it sparingly and do it only with an exclamation point. Don't be tempted to underline.

WAS is too often the determiner of the passive voice and as mentioned earlier writers must watch for it with Sherlock's magnifying glass. It was a dark and stormy night. (smile here) Passive. A storm roared through the dark night. Active. Jennifer was speaking quietly. Passive. Jennifer spoke quietly. Active. As discussed in Chapter Four, don't forget that when you finish each chapter of your novel, go to the Find feature and enter "was" to help you locate passives sentences you didn't realize you'd written. More than likely there will be some. Or many.

THERE dulls prose down to a crawl and is usually followed by WAS, the passive drudge. There was a light in the distance. We have just been told something. Dull and passive. A light appeared in the distance. We just saw a light. Interesting and active.

WOULD is another deadener to be wary of in your writing. It is in the conditional case under grammar rules although it actually refers to tense. Example: He would usually phone her at two in the afternoon. Afterward he would stop for a late lunch and then kill time until he would stop by her house around five. Would-would-would tells us what he does but is boring - and passive. Write actively, showing him calling her at two in the afternoon, maybe qualifying his actions with "as he did daily" or something to imply the regularity of his actions.

Gerunds are verbs ending in "ing" used to start a sentence. "Running after the metro train, Peter knew that if he was late for the meeting he could kiss his job goodbye." Sentences structured such as this have long been frowned upon, but times do change. We see these more regularly now in fiction. They work if used frugally. Very many of these and readers react. Not positively, sorry to say.

SERMONS. Leave the sermons and moralizing to the church pulpits. Readers aren't giving you their time and interest to be preached to and you should know when you are doing it. I believe the only 'sermon' I ever read that I thought was good writing and worth reading was short and was in one of James Michener's novels, though I don't recall which one. Maybe *Tales of the South Pacific*.

But then Michener can write an interesting sentence that runs on for two pages. I've never tried it and don't necessarily recommend that you do either.

CLICHES. Avoid them. They smack of mediocrity. You will run into them in your own fiction reading but that doesn't mean you should use them. Strive to do better. If you can't think of a sharp metaphor or simile, rewrite the sentence without one. Or if you have come to a perfect place to use a cliché, then alter it slightly which readers appreciate. Instead of "quiet as a mouse" try "quiet as a breeze" or "as a butterfly." (The best one I heard was "quiet as a broken clock.") I once wrote "as the crow flies." Immediately I knew that was no good but when I amended it to "as the barn swallow flies," it worked.

REDUNDANCIES. A sentence that contains superfluous words whose meaning is already conveyed is a redundant one. Leonard Bishop, in his book *Dare To Be a Great Writer,* points out the sloppiness of redundancies. He gives this example: "Surrounded on all sides." You cannot be surrounded on three sides. "Surrounded" is sufficient. Other examples are: I just got a PC computer. Redundant. A PC is a computer. The decision was completely unanimous. No, unanimous is complete. I once read "That was a false lie!" Uh, what? Watch for your own redundant sentences. It is surprisingly easy to fall into writing them. I've written my share.

Bishop also quoted Mark Twain on a similar problem: "The difference between the right word and the almost right word is the difference between lightning and the lightning bug."

Act Two is the landscape of your story. Here is where you will need all your knowledge on writing. In addition to the techniques discussed in this chapter you should be able to easily handle Flashbacks, Foreshadowing, Scene Structure, Style and Pacing. The more you study and learn technique the better writer you will become.

⚓〜Seven〜⚓

How to Develop Your Style

What exactly is Style? Basically it has to do with the way a writer puts his words together. It isn't just what he says, it's how he says it. Author Gary Provost in his little gem of a book, *Make Every Word Count*, talks about excerpts from two books he looked at regarding the human brain. He randomly opened one and read this sentence:

"But does the greater spontaneity and speed of assimilatory coordination between schemata fully explain the internalization of behavior, or does representation begin at the present level, thus indicating the transition from sensori-motor intelligence to genuine thought?"

He opened the second book and pointed a finger. This is what he read:

"If a frog's eyes are rotated 180 degrees, it will move its tongue in the wrong direction for food and will literally starve to death as a result of the inability to compensate for the distortion."

Provost asks, "Which book do you think I read? Which book would you have read?"

He points out that the second book uses visual images to convey what that author understands into a language the reader can understand. We can transfer that same analysis into fiction and show the effect it has on style.

Certain writers come to mind immediately when considering style. Ernest Hemingway is one of the standard bearers. A passage read out of context is recognizable as his work. So is the case with two of my favorites, James A Michener and James Lee Burke. When reading those authors it is not uncommon for a writer to suck in his breath and think, Why couldn't I have said that? Writing teachers frequently refer to Tom Wolfe and his shout-out style. Others with distinctive styles are Raymond Chandler and the watershed detective writer, Mickey Spillane and his hard-boiled crime protagonist, Mike Hammer. In 1947, newly married Spillane is said to have needed money to buy a house. He wrote *I, The Jury* in nineteen days and sent it to E. P. Dalton. It became an international best seller with six and a half million copies selling in the U.S. alone. Spillane set the stage for that genre forever after, his style being the prototype for future detective crime writers.

Previously we talked about adjectives and adverbs. When a writer packs his work with them they become clutter. Hemingway's style is distinctive because of how tightly he writes. He pares sentences down to the core. Eliminate every single adjective and adverb in the novel you are working on and you still will not be Hemingway. But if you avoid flamboyancy and tighten your writing, your own style will begin to surface.

There are two steps to writing tightly. The first is to weed out the fluff. After you've plucked out the adjectives and adverbs, look for the unnecessary words and sentences. This includes redundancy and side roads you might have taken that sounded good at the time but actually only bog down the story. Wordiness also includes those long passages of exposition. Get rid of them. Exposition passages 'tell' the story and you already know that your mission is to show, not tell. Write in the active voice, that is to say, make your sentences active, not passive.

Earlier, we discussed some examples. Here are a few more. Your character says, "I know a woman who is mean." What if your character says, "I know a woman who beats her dog with a board until he howls." In the first sentence we heard what the character said. We may have conjured a vague mental picture of some sort of mean woman. In the second we again heard the character but we also saw the woman beating her dog, we heard the animal's howls of pain and our emotions were immediately engaged. While more words were utilized in the second example they were words that deliver. They had an impact on us as well as providing information. You could write, "The wind was blowing strong." A stronger sentence is "The wind ripped the old door from its hinges with a metallic screech."

The second step to eliminate wordiness is to avoid or delete pretentious words. Don't use a hundred dollar word when a moderately-priced one would be better. Quoting author Gary Provost again, look at this paragraph from what he calls his "short lived novel, *'The Rabbit Knows.'*"

"So he stood torpidly on the pebbled border of the lifeless highway with his arm outstretched across the corroded asphalt and his thumb sought some sort of concession to his distress, and once again he found himself making nugatory conjectures."

Zzzzz. The sentence is bad enough, but torpidly? Puh-leeze. And do you know what "nugatory conjectures" are? I'd be happy to tell you, but I'd have to go to my dictionary first. One look at that paragraph and both agents and readers would surely say, Nope, don't think so. Plunk. File 13.

When a writer uses uncommon, pretentious words because he thinks it will make him sound educated and sophisticated, he achieves strained, pretentious paragraphs. His writing suffers. He won't grow into a writer with the kind of personal style that draws readers to his work.

Another caveat is to be specific. If you're writing about your character, instead of saying his hands, say his long-fingered hands. Not his eyes, but his heavy-lidded eyes. He doesn't go to a bar, he goes to the ginmill down on 3rd Street. Don't have him see just any house, but rather a specific house—a bungalow or a mansion or a chalet. Instead of referring to his wit, talk about his ascetic wit or his dry humor. Specifics have the impact on your reader of helping her to get inside the character's skin, experience the scene, feel the story.

A writer's style develops as he involves himself in the discipline. He becomes a writer, a better writer, a great writer, by this triangle: writing, reading and studying the techniques of the craft of writing. Ignoring any one of these three components will impact progress. The most difficult task a writer will face is to write. The easiest is to stare at the computer, go make a sandwich, phone a friend or any other avoidance behavior at which he is proficient. To become a writer you must write. You need to do it every day. When you finish one project you must start another. Stepping away from writing "for a break" is a dangerous decision. A day becomes a week which becomes a month and beyond.

That is not to say that an author who has just finished the final edit of his novel, an impressive undertaking by anyone's yardstick, must immediately start another. A break or a vacation could certainly be warranted. Sometimes we do have to rest and recharge before we are ready to take on our next major task. But a re-energizing period should not be of any substantial length.

Gymnasts and runners who have stepped away for a break report how quickly they lose their momentum. In more ways than one. Almost all will mention focus, of course, but they also speak of muscle. The muscles called upon for their particular sport start breaking down from disuse. Equally important, the person loses muscle memory, critical to athletes. When they return to their workouts and training, they do not return in the same condition. It takes work to get back to the point at which they stopped. The same can be applied to writers. Step away too long and you will lose focus, momentum and creative muscle memory.

The second component of developing as a writer is to read. Some writers say they cannot read while they are involved with their own work. I hope that is not the case for you. Reading is part of the triangle and if you set aside a time each day to read you will find that the activity keeps you in a literary frame of mind. Sometimes, as you read, new ideas will occur to you for your own story. I like to keep a pen and paper beside me when I read. I never know what is going to suddenly pop up and thump me. Try not to convince yourself that you don't have the time. If you examine your daily routine you will find several ways to gather in reading time. One is to give up an hour or so of watching television. TV does not stimulate the literary juices; it is passive entertainment. If you argued that reading is passive entertainment, too, you'd be wrong. Not in the case of a writer. When a writer reads he gains more than just being entertained; he learns. You don't even have to concentrate on how the author handles his 'style,' you absorb details and technique while you are actually focused on the story itself. Nor do you have to read the same genre you write. If your novels are crime thrillers but you enjoy sci-fi, read it. If you write romance but love to curl up with a good who-done-it, by all means read that. Read novels in your own genre, too. You want to know how other authors approach your favored category. Reading has another interesting benefit. It rests your mind while it entertains you.

The third part of the literary triangle, learning the craft of writing, is self-explanatory. It's why you are reading this book. Don't neglect continuing to learn the craft.

It's important as you develop as a writer that you do not get over-analytical and thus mechanical. Let your writing flow from you. You can, and will, make needed adjustments during rewriting. For now, put your backside into the chair, turn on the computer and write.

Style, specifically in the viewpoint of agents and editors, includes grammar. And that includes spelling, punctuation, sentence structure and more. Even if you intend to hire an editor to 'fix all that' you, as a professional writer, ought to know how to spell and use basic punctuation. And you certainly need to know how to put a sentence together so it says what you want it to say. *Strunk & White's Elements of Style* should be one of your good friends, as said in early chapters. This little ninety-page book is packed with easy to locate rules.

Author William Zinsser said, "Writing is an act of ego and we might as well admit it." I agree. Believe in yourself, be confident, attend to the three parts of your triangle, and your signature, your style, will emerge.

❧ ⌘⌘ ❧

ᛗᛗ~~~Eight~~~ᛗᛗ

How to Create Memorable Characters

Stories are said to be either plot driven or character driven. Plot driven novels like thrillers, disasters and war, tend to focus on events, action, getting out of danger. If we want to tell a story, we must have a storyline, that's a given. But if we just drop our story people into the landscape in order to further the plot, it is too easy to leave them as 'cardboard characters.' How you develop, or don't develop, your characters will determine if they are round or flat.

Flat characters always damage a book and frequently ruin one. Whether a story is character driven or plot driven, a writer has a serious problem if his readers don't care about the people in the story. A good beginning might have 'hooked' them in but it won't take them long to lose interest in the whole book if they don't get involved in the lives of the characters. They bought your book but if they don't like it or don't even finish it, they won't be in line for your future writings and they won't bring their friends along either. In fiction, word of mouth is the number one reason people buy books. Someone told them what a great read a book is and when they are in a bookstore, book section of the supermarket or online, they will look for something familiar to read. A majority of the time it will be a novel recommended to them.

It is tremendously difficult to break out of the huge number of offerings that are in the Internet stores. There is said to be in excess of a million books available on Amazon and large numbers are uploaded daily. What does a writer have to do to be noticed?

Social networking is demanded of writers today whether traditionally or independently published, but a poorly written book doesn't stand much of a chance, no matter how hard the author works at marketing. We've already agreed that the beginning must grab a reader and keep him reading into the night. But if your characters are wooden and unbelievable, the reader will have a hard time staying with you, and many won't.

Where to start? When a character appears in a novel, we, as writers, must get into that character's head. We must become him, at least while he is on stage. If there are twenty characters then we'll have to slip into the persona of each of them. Be the fiancée while she is in the scene, think like she does, speak as she would. Be the gardener. Be the neighbor.

When creating the character in your reader's eye, it will be tempting to write something like, "She was exceptionally tall for a woman, close to six feet. She was thin with long fingers and had red hair. Her eyes were hazel and more oval than round. She had a long slender nose and full lips. She was a cautious, non-trusting type." Sad to say many writers fall into this easy method of describing a character. A better and more effective way is to flesh out the character as the storyline progresses. Have someone else notice or comment on her height. A waitress could stare at her red hair. The character's own actions and dialogue can let us know that she does not trust people. Develop her as the story moves forward.

Remind yourself, too, that less is more. Readers bring their own experiences to a novel. The writer can be minimal in his descriptions of a character. The reader will fill in what the writer leaves out and readers will visualize your story people. Interestingly, they won't all see her the same.

NAMES

Give your characters tags and traits or at least give them to your major characters. We've briefly discussed giving your characters names and they're all going to need one. Maybe not a shopkeeper referred to briefly in the book as 'the shopkeeper,' but the rest of them will. You may not know right off what name is right for a particular character even your protagonist. If you feel you have given him the wrong name, you can refer to him by his role or his temperament, such as "Don't make it your business," Grumpy said, or Protagonist said or Builder said. At some point you are either going to feel the right name, your character will tell you his name or you'll go on a Google search looking for a name that will suit him.

While writing *Destinies*, I was well into the character of the ship captain's daughter but she wasn't moving along well for me. I figured out that she was wearing the wrong name. When I changed her name she came alive. After that, whenever she was in a scene, she spoke naturally, acted in accordance with who she was. She played her part and I became the scribe, capturing what she did and said.

If a difficult great-aunt is named Jennifer, she isn't going to feel right to your readers and she won't feel right to you, either. You probably won't find her easy to write. But change her name to Hortense or even Cordelia and watch her start to take on a life. A sweet, scatterbrained great-auntie named Gertie will most likely have you smiling as you allow her to play her part with hands that flutter around blue hair while she gives off the scents of talcum powder and old lace.

A word of warning: avoid giving your people sound alike names. You don't want your female characters to be named Betty, Barbara, Beth, Bonnie and Bernadette. If you read The Brothers Karamazov you probably remember, with agony, the challenge of keeping all the characters straight. Think carefully, too, before you tag your characters with names from highly read books, current or past. It's difficult to give your characters personalities of their own if you use names like Hermione, Hamlet, Scarlet or Spock.

TRAITS

Characters, main ones especially, should have traits
that the reader becomes familiar with. For a character
with a slight limp, the first time it is mentioned briefly
describe how that limp came about. You could have one
character explain it to another. As the detective walks
away, someone comments on the limp and the detective's
partner says, "Yeah, a souvenir he brought home from
Nam, compliments of the Viet Cong." Or for a younger
detective, adjust that to Afghanistan, compliments of the
Taliban. Later in your story have the detective on the job
thirteen hours, exhausted, and this time show the limp as
more pronounced.

Any trait you give a character should not be
overwritten. Mention it a few times spaced throughout
the story. When you show it the second time, your reader
will attach it to that character and by the time you write it
again the reader will know which character it is even if
you do not name him directly. "A man with his jacket
collar turned up limped toward the house." We know
who's coming. If your character has a habit, show that a

bit more often. If he loves lifesavers, have him pop one into his mouth frequently. The nervous woman who twirls a strand of hair should be seen to do that at appropriate times.

You may also use repetition of an object belonging to the character to have a dramatizing effect. In the *#1 Ladies Detective Agency*, and into the next books of the series, Mme Ramotswe's vehicle is a tiny white van in which she drives around the South African countryside doing her detecting. We hear about it frequently but it is never described as a vehicle or just a van. It is always a "tiny white van." If you want to read story-telling at its best, see at least this first book in author Alexander McCall Smith's "Ladies Detective Agency" series.

Be careful about making a trait comedic; frequent use can do that. You are writing a novel, not the dialogue for a cartoon. Sylvester the Cat can get away with saying "Thufferin' Thuccotash" repeatedly, but your lisping or stuttering character cannot.

THE FIVE SENSES

When we consider how much each of the five senses contributes to bringing fictional characters to life, it is disconcerting that writers repeatedly ignore three of them. We see, hear, touch, smell and taste. We also possess a sixth sense not so easy to label so we simply call it sixth sense. In its developed stage it is referred to, or claimed as, extrasensory perception. Whatever it is and whatever label we give it, it is an effective tool to have in our writing bag of tricks. Don't be afraid to use it.

Sight and sound are the most common senses writers use, but a story is improved when smell, taste and touch are employed. Incorporate them and your character is rounder, fuller and we as readers see and identify with him more deeply.

Of the five senses, which do you think has the most impact? If you guessed Smell you'd be right. You might describe a man's aversion to taking baths and the reader could form his mental picture from that. But the reader's own senses are called into play if she reads that the man smelled of unwashed clothing and ripe armpits. The writer has the power to have the reader inhaling the sweet scents of an orange grove, or a lilac tree, the odor of a diaper pail or the fresh cow pie the barefoot character just stepped into. In the case of the cow pie, as readers we not only smell that, we also can feel it between our toes.

In *A Free Man of Color*, author Barbara Hambly tell us that her protagonist, January, has been put into a cell with two mulattos, an old drunk white man, two cots with flat straw mattresses and a bucket. She writes:

"Roaches the length of January's thumb scampered over the sleeper and in and out of mattresses, bucket and the cracks in the walls. His palms felt damp, and he wiped them on torn and dirty trousers.

"The white man spat. Daubs and squiggles of expectorated tobacco juice covered the wall opposite him and the floor beneath. The sweetish, greasy stench of it rivaled the smell of the bucket."

Do you see that scene? Feel it? Smell it? This is good writing and powerful use of the senses.

DIALOG

How a person speaks, which we touched on earlier, is critical in character development. Dialog comes easy to some writers, not so to others. Develop an ear for speech by listening to how people speak, their expressions and patterns, the rhythm of speech.

Fiction dialog, however, is not a transcript of how people actually talk. But when we write it, and when it is read, it must sound real. Dialog that is stilted, forced or flat is a story killer. We're not writing an elementary primer. We need to give a character words and sentences he would say, taking into account how we are developing him.

We want a character to talk in a manner that fits who he is in the story. A person from Boston is not going to sound the same as one from Alabama. A Boston hoodlum will not speak the same as a doctor from the same city. As much as their accents, what they say is important to fleshing out the character. We know that a professional will choose different words and have different expressions than a working man and they will be different yet again from a criminal. Let the dialog fit the character.

In Lawrence Block's Matt Scudder series, Matt has a friend, Mick Ballou, who is a criminal, a rather hard-core one at that. Not only does Block develop this hood so that we like him but we also know that he is Irish. Block uses just enough idioms and dialect to keep us aware of Mick's Irish-ness. He does not beat us over the head with it, which is important to take note of.

The same is true of the characters in Kathryn Stockett's *The Help*. Aibileen, Minny and their friends, all speak with only the slightest patois to their speech. Listen to the dialect in this passage:

"Aibileen says nothing for a while. Keeps peeling tomatoes around and around. 'He read this book call *Invisible Man*. When he done, he say he gone write down what it was like to be colored working for a white man in Mississippi.'"

Notice how she says *call* for called. Not he's done, but *he done*, and *he gone* write. Throughout the book Aibileen and Minny rarely say 'is' and by that omission her speech pattern becomes notably different from the dialog of the white employers. Aibileen also says *on* in place of 'going to' all through the story, a small word that has an impact on us as readers. Here she is about to tell a story to the little girl she takes care of:

"Today I'm on tell you bout a man from outer space."

The author does not load the book with black patois but rather uses a few specific words and phrases that make us believe we are hearing a dialect of southern black people. The same can be done with dialogue for any character, whether he is from Maine or Massachusetts, Mississippi or Montana and whether he's a horse trader in 1840 Kansas or a thoroughbred owner in 2012 Kentucky. Use a light touch to draw your characters without overloading them with dialect that wearies the reader.

We've been discussing the quality of dialogue but a word needs to be said about quantity. When a reader picks up a book and thumbs through it, we already know he is not going to be attracted by pages of exposition. Good writers do make use of description, but it's a given that it must not run on and on. The same is true when a character is speaking. If he goes on too long, it becomes a speech and any longer it turns into a lecture. We like dialogue and as writers we want to use a lot of it in our novels. The solution is to have interruptions in what your character is saying. The person he's speaking to might pose a question or interrupt with comments of his own. The speaker might interrupt himself by getting up and pouring a glass of water or maybe making a "wait a second" sign with one finger as he answers a ringing phone. Or maybe other characters appear on the scene or in some way the story interrupts him. Similarly, dialogue that goes on too long between two or more people can put a reader off.

Early on we said that one good method of writing is to start at the beginning and go forward, not stopping to correct or rewrite. This has an added benefit in that by the time you finish the first draft and go back for the all important first rewrite, if you come on five pages of straight dialogue you can be sure it is going to have you

shaking your head and saying, "Oh oh, did I write that?"
Now that you recognize the problem it is relatively easy
to fix with appropriate interruptions and side roads and
still end up with the entire dialogue intact.

GOALS AND OBSTACLES

For us to care about a character that person has to
care about something himself. His wants and goals are
the underpinnings of your story. In the chapter on
plotting, we saw that obstacles are part of the plot format.
No matter what conflicts come up for your character, his
goal must remain foremost in his mind and must
influence his actions. If he overcomes one hurdle he must
come up against another in its place. Solving one issue
may give rise to one he hadn't anticipated. The more he
has to deal with opposition to his desires, the more
determined he must become to succeed. We already
know that when all obstacles are resolved, the story is
over. Keep one roadblock after another impeding his
progress while he refuses to give up. Turn up the heat,
make it seem impossible for him to succeed but keep
telling us that he believes he can. When your character

cares and his words and actions show that he cares, we in turn care about him.

Our love of characters has had us sitting in front of our TV sets once a week for years—from characters like Gunsmoke's Matt Dillon back in the day to The Big Bang Theory's Bernadette Rostenkowski recently. Most of our favorite novels bring to mind our favorite characters as well; Katniss Everdeen, Jacob Jankowski, Hermione Granger, Alex Cross and more. Know your characters intimately. Know what they would do in a variety of circumstances, even if those scenes won't be used in your book. The better you know your people the more alive they will be in the story.

And the more memorable.

❦ ~~~Nine~~~ ❦

How to Handle Suspense and Foreshadowing

When we hear the word Suspense in conjunction with fiction we tend to conjure up visions of the infamous dark and stormy night, the heroine home alone, the telephone out of order - and oh-my-God what are those scratching sounds? Is someone trying to open a window? Eeuu, shivering chills down the spine.

Suspense, however, does not have to be that dramatic to keep readers turning the pages. Whenever there is a hint that something is going to happen, that hint creates a measure of suspense. Writing suspense fiction and writing suspense into fiction are not the same.

Suspense, or Thriller/Suspense, is a genre that immediately speaks of danger. Our main character is facing a crisis, perhaps disaster, maybe even death. Or the entire society is at risk of annihilation. In Thriller/Suspense stories the stakes are extremely high and the tension becomes excruciating. The entire story is focused on fear and danger. Think *Mission Impossible II, Mulholland Drive, Before the Devil Knows You're Dead, The Girl Who Kicked the Hornet's Nest, Independence Day*. The movie *Titanic* is classified as Drama genre, but it is suspense clear through. And who could ever forget *Psycho*?

However, stories in other genres must also have tension and suspense built in if they are going to be successful. That is what keeps readers turning pages. *Water for Elephants* is Drama or Literary Fiction, but both the book and the movie are strongly filled with suspense. There is always a question in front of us as to what is going to happen next.

That, in fact, is the key to suspense: What happens next?

Whenever you give your character a problem, your reader becomes engaged and wants to know how or if the character can solve it. Raise the character's anxieties and the reader becomes anxious as well. Maybe your character has to make a choice between two situations, both of which he wants. Or maybe he's really up against it, the natives are swooping down on him and his only way out is to leap off the cliff into the river far below. In scenarios like these, you have to plan ahead for your resolutions. Please do not resort to the cavalry type rescue. Readers will not forgive you.

You can build tremendous tension by piling one problem after another onto your protagonist. As soon as he figures a way to resolve one issue, hit him with another one. But only do it if he can find his way through each dilemma and the reader can believe it.

Suspense is also built when the reader knows something the protagonist doesn't. Tension increases for the reader as the character is unable to resolve the problem, or when he stumbles into a new problem, or when there is serious danger ahead of which the reader is aware but the character isn't. The reader identifies with the character, or at least cares about him in scenarios like these and that is exactly what we want.

Writers want to keep in mind that a problem doesn't have to be monumental. Stories don't need a monster shark like Jaws or a ripper like Jack to bring about tension. The movie Fatal Attraction, although a script not a book, has about as much tension and suspense as one person can endure. Even our childhood stories were filled with suspense. Jack is climbing the beanstalk? Oh no, what's up there?

Unpredictable events add to tension. Difficulties arise, hence suspense. Expectations don't happen, hence tension. Something terrible is going to happen to the character if he doesn't get this or that done by a known deadline – nail-biting suspense. Even hilarious lightweights like *Summer Breeze* by Mary Kay Andrews keep us engaged with fast paced complications that make us ask, what happens next?

Remind yourself as you write that your mission is to beat up your protagonist, make mountains out of molehills by turning small problems into blocks that prevent him from reaching his goal. Make the odds seem impossible. Just as he's overcoming one obstacle, throw up another one. You don't have to be writing thrillers to do this (though it certainly works well in that genre.) Use this technique in your story whether it is romance, paranormal, sci-fi, mystery or any other genre. If your work starts to feel flat, look to your characters. Are things too easy for your protagonist? Is your antagonist weak? If so, better haul out the tried and true techniques of torturing your character, make that antagonist a certifiable pain in the neck or make him violent or make him sleazy, slimy or sneaky. Pump up the suspense until the reader won't be able to put the novel down. Suspense makes for page-turning books.

Possibly you've heard that foreshadowing creates suspense. Maybe you've asked yourself, what is foreshadowing? If you're a reader, and you should be if you intend to be a good writer, you have already come across this literary device for creating suspense.

Foreshadowing is powerful – it has major importance in story telling but is somewhat challenging to learn. According to Merriam-Webster, to foreshadow is to represent, typify or indicate beforehand. Their example is: Her early interest in airplanes foreshadowed her later career as a pilot. But foreshadowing in fiction is much stronger than that dictionary sentence. It is related to foretelling in that they both predict. Foreshadow, of course, is considerably more discreet and not in the mystic realm.

Readers and writers alike are aware of Chekov's famous gun in the first act. It is often referenced in discussions of foreshadowing. The idea is that if someone gets shot in the third act, the gun had better be shown in the first one. Or reversed theory: If a gun is hanging on the wall in the first act, it should go off in the next act. If it isn't going to be used, it shouldn't be hanging there.

You can show an apparently unimportant object early in the story that will later become significant. A comment can be made that will have meaning later. As the story rushes along, foreshadow can become foreboding— making the reader feel uneasy even though she doesn't know why. Foreshadowing whether by description or dialog should be relatively transparent and should be written into the story a bit at a time. Your reader sees it but doesn't focus on it until much later when she realizes that there were clues early on about the event that just occurred.

Many writers find that foreshadowing is too difficult to work out while writing the rough first draft. After a revision or two as the story comes together you can go back and write in foreshadowing where it will enhance the suspense of the story. At this point 'red herrings' can be added. These are clues or foreshadow pointing to the wrong character or the wrong outcome. Even the character can get it wrong and focus on the red herring. Of course these must be corrected later on in a way that the reader can accept. You've seen it regularly in other books; you can do it in yours, too.

There are two things about foreshadowing that a writer must remember. One is to not focus on something that won't show up again in the story. It leaves readers confused and unsatisfied. If you put emphasis on a guitar standing in the corner, but nothing in the story ever relates back to the guitar, you will have an unhappy reader.

The second to keep in mind is that you must not give too much away at one time. If you do, you have killed the suspense instead of adding to it.

The use of foreshadowing and the techniques of suspense should not overwhelm you. Write both into your fiction repeatedly. You will get better at it as you use them. It is a given that they will improve your story and contribute to your being a better writer.

It has been estimated that it takes 10,000 hours to perfect anything – gymnastics, tennis, ice skating, music, art, singing, writing. . .

Maybe you'd better get busy.

❧⊶ℭ℞℘℔⊷❧

How to End Your Novel

You have used all your skills to keep the reader turning pages through the beginning and middle of your novel. We established the proportions of a novel to be smaller beginning and endings, the largest section being the middle. In the beginning, or Act I, you set the hook, labored to make the first paragraphs pull the reader in, introduced at least one character and the first of the conflicts your book will contain. The middle, Act II, the largest portion of the book, has the reader involved in the lives of the characters and crashing into one problem/conflict/obstruction after another as the story develops and mounts in tension.

As you come to the ending of the novel you are required – yes, required – to deliver a satisfying ending. The reader's emotional commitment must be addressed. When the last page is read, the end must be believable and acceptable even if she might wish it had ended differently for your characters.

Give thought to every unresolved situation that is occurring in the book, the conflict or obstruction for your main character and every problem that exists for each minor character. Remember that we have talked before about every character having at least one problem, even if not earth-shattering. Each of those problems must be resolved in some manner or they will be the loose ends that will damage your book. They will generate negative thoughts in your reader's mind and may even translate into negative reviews or comments to friends. That is the last thing you want. Don't let a badly written, poorly designed conclusion diminish or even destroy your novel.

How to accomplish a good ending? Start with resolving the problems and obstacles of your lesser characters as you work toward the end of Act II and the first part of Act III. Resolve the least of these first; leave the important issues intact for your reader to focus on and worry about.

An ending has two parts, the climax and the denouement. Throughout the story you have set up the conflicts, you have engaged the emotions of the reader, you have built the suspense. The climax must reach the highest point of that conflict and suspense—and solve it to the reader's emotional satisfaction. Consider this: if you've written a very large book, the climax will be longer than in a shorter novel or a short story.

This is the highest point of tension or drama in your novel and you want to deal with it in a way that is realistic, which is to say that you must involve the characters that already live in its pages. Keep third party saviors out of the mix. If Superman shows up on the scene or the cavalry rides in just in the nick of time, trust me, your readers will not speak kindly of your novel and they won't read your next work. Such a climax is neither logical nor believable. If your story met its promise of change, then your characters will not only resolve the issues, they will not be the same people they were at the beginning of the story. Changes do not have to be monumental. Most will have grown and learned. Some will not.

Scarlet O'Hara did not grow, she did not learn, she was the same self-serving person at the end of *Gone with the Wind* as she was at the beginning. But Rhett changed, other characters changed, the war changed the nation. The book worked and it worked well.

What ending is the right one? Only the author can decide that even if a reader might have preferred a different one or thinks she knows a better one. The writer, in fact, should consider a variety of endings to come up with the best and most suitable one. Often we see a movie ending that differs from the original book. Sometimes the ending is better and sometimes not. The point is, though, the screenwriter saw more than one possible ending.

The Firm, John Grisham's runaway bestseller, was a highly successful movie that earned Two Hundred Seventy Million Dollars worldwide, a substantial figure for 1993. In the movie, Mitch, the protagonist, solves his crisis in a different manner than in the book. Although I loved the book, I personally liked the movie ending much better. It was more pleasing and certainly more believable. No offense intended, Mr. Grisham.

In *The Help*, while there were a variety of minor differences, the solution to Minny's problem with her abusive husband is far better portrayed in the book. In fact, the book wins all the way round. *Water for Elephants*—same thing. While it is considered an excellent movie it could not capture the emotional impact of the book or the depth of the characters, good or evil.

You, as author, not only build the book, write and design the story and characters, you have the choice of how to end it. How big or how long to make the climax, whether it is going to be all sweetness and roses and if your protagonist is going to win or lose are choices you must make. Take care in considering the potential possibilities. Of course, if a movie house takes an option screenwriters might change your story anyway. Don't be sad. Be comforted all the way to the bank and know that a lot of movie viewers will then go buy your book. And probably say it was better than the movie.

Whatever ending you decide on, decide something. Do not be inconclusive. Readers do not like an unresolved, open-ended novel. They don't want to figure it out for themselves. Readers come to be entertained, to be told a story and that includes a beginning, a middle and an ending. If you went to a play, thoroughly enjoying Act I and Act II, but when the curtain rose on Act III instead of the players there was a big sign on stage that said, "Guess!" how would you react? That play might have been Neil Simon at his best for two acts, but you would have gone away saying bad things about him and his abilities as a writer. Do your readers a favor—write a complete novel for them. Don't leave the ending vague.

The denouement is everything that comes after the climax. Write your climax too quickly, resolve all the issues and your book is essentially over. When you do have the climax in place you have only a little more of your reader's attention for the denouement, so be sure you are ready for the climax and have written one the reader finds satisfying. Then you can finish with the denouement where you can tell, briefly, what happened with the characters whose lives weren't resolved in the climax. You can also write brief consequences of the storyline or plot. Readers like that.

There does not have to be a denouement, often there isn't and almost never in a short story. But in novels of any length the author will usually add to the climactic scene. Readers find that satisfactory or even comforting. It gives them closure to the story. Do, however, make it brief. Drama is good, too, just be sure it is less dramatic than the climax.

An epilogue, like a prologue, is the author's choice. My epic novel, Destinies, is an historical drama set in the eighteenth century when Catherine seizes the crown of Russia and a thousand miles away a Rhineland boy's life changes forever. The novel actually ends with the last chapter. I chose to write an epilogue because while Christian's story was resolved, I believed, rightly so by the mail from readers, that people might want to know Catherine's fate. Not many are knowledgeable about her or her country during her reign. The most that is generally known about Russia's czars is the name of Peter the Great and the slaughter of the last czar, Nicholas Romanov and his family during the Bolshevik Revolution. The epilogue in Destinies gives the fate of Catherine and to my relief readers have found it fulfilling. If you have a similar situation in your novel, consider an epilogue, or an epilogue and author's note for the benefit of your reader.

Endings are not easy. They must answer each and every question the story brings to a reader's mind. Check the obstacles you've set up in your novel and make certain that they have all been overcome.

More is available in books and articles about writing beginnings and middles than is taught on producing good endings. Work diligently on producing yours because it will either complete or damage your book. When you started writing you didn't know what hard work writing a full-length book was going to be. Don't allow a weak ending to diminish your quality novel.

☜~~~Eleven~~~☞

Odds and Ends

As we near the end it's time to squeeze in some bits and pieces that haven't been touched on, or were touched on only lightly.

SETTING. Let's look at setting through a writer's eyes. Setting gives us the opportunity to create a scene and to initiate action. You can use a setting, a park or an airport for example, as the stage for your characters or for plot movement. Let's say your protagonist, Jill, and her friend, Ted, have to be at a hospital at a certain time for an incident that must occur in the plot. To set up our situation, we could have them walk through a park. An elderly lady puts her package on the end of a bench and it falls off. As she tries to catch it she loses her balance and crashes to the sidewalk. Ted sprints across the park to help the woman. She appears to have injured, possibly broken, her arm. Ted dials 911 on his cell phone. Jill rushes across the grass to where the woman is weeping.

She is afraid to go in the ambulance, but Ted holds her hand and assures her that he will ride with her to be certain that everything goes all right. Jill will drive his car to the hospital.

Now let's arrange for a different plot and a different plot need. Let's say that this same couple is at an airport, going through a checkpoint. Ted is stopped when the buzzer sounds. He is asked to step out of line and remove his ring and bracelet, empty his pockets. A security agent begins going over his body with a hand held metal detector. The body-check goes on for what Ted feels is an unreasonably long time. He reacts angrily, makes a scene, and protests loudly that the agent has singled him out. Then he claims the man touched his private body parts. The agent is offended and Jill is embarrassed.

The reader is introduced to two quite different characters that the settings helped to create. In the first scenario the writer uses the park and an accident to show Ted as a caring person while also getting the couple to the hospital for plot development.

In the second scene, it is the airport that is used to set up a situation. The couple moves on and the subject is dropped. The story continues. But the reader has had a glimpse of Ted's short fuse. She sees that he reacts inappropriately to the situation. The writer has used the location and surroundings to develop a scene hinting at the character's temper that will surface later in the story.

When you use settings in your novels avoid descriptions of places the reader already knows. In the above examples, you don't need to describe the park, we all know what a park looks like. Since this park isn't intrinsic to the plot, we need not go into detail as to its layout or amenities nor do we need to describe the airport. Most everyone has been in an airport and anyone who hasn't has probably seen one on television or in a movie. Again, the airport is only a setting the writer is using to expose his character's bad disposition.

SENTENCE STRUCTURE. Strange as it might sound, when a book begins to feel tedious to a reader, it may not be due to poor plot or dull characters. The reason could be repetitious sentence lengths. Writers sometimes get into habits that they are not aware of. That is especially true of same-length sentences. Sentences that are consistently eight words long, or four or forty, become tiresome after awhile. The reader begins to feel uncomfortable. Perhaps she has trouble with her concentration and may put the book down to go do something else. It takes longer for the reader to become aware of her discomfort when she is reading routine length sentences than it does reading the repeated use of a writer's favorite word. The fourth or fifth time the writer uses "supposedly," for example, the reader tunes in to it. But she isn't as quick to see same-length sentences. She will feel the effects but more than likely would not be able to explain them.

The solution to this is to vary your sentences. Write sentences with different numbers of words. Write simple sentences, such as: Most boys want to have a dog. (The sentence contains a noun and a verb.) Write compound sentences, such as: Jennie liked to read romance novels but her friend preferred paranormal stories. (The sentence contains two independent clauses, connected by 'but.') Connectors are but, or, and, yet, so, for and nor.

Write complex sentences, such as: Jeff and Tonya went dancing after they finished eating dinner. Here is something interesting to consider about complex sentences. Look at this sentence: After they finished eating dinner, Jeff and Tonya went dancing. Compare it with the previous sentence. What is the difference between the two? In the first example, the sentence starts with the action: "Jeff and Tonya went dancing" and the reader feels the action through the entire sentence. In the second, the sentence begins with the dependent clause therefore requiring a comma: "After they finished eating dinner," – the comma creates a brief pause in the reader's mind. Further, the action has been moved to the end of the sentence.

The complex sentence is indeed complex. Here is one description: A complex sentence has an independent clause joined by one or more dependent clauses. It always has a subordinator such as: because, since, after, although, or when or a relative pronoun such as that, who, or which.

As you change the length and type of your sentences, you might even become as good a writer as Tolkien. In Return of the King, Sam sprang out to meet Shagrat: "He was no longer holding the ring, but it was there, a hidden power, a cowing menace to the slaves of Mordor, and in his hand was Sting, and its light smote the eyes of the orc—" and on and on before we see a period. The total number of words in that Tolkien sentence? Seventy.

If sentence structure is not clear to a writer, it is in his best interests to buy a good grammar book such as *Baron's Painless Grammar* by Rebecca Elliot PhD or *The Blue Book of Grammar* by Jane Straus. Don't just buy it, study it. An understanding of grammar is one of the essential items in a writer's toolbox. Rules can be bent or broken, but a writer should know what the rules are before attempting to change them. Good writing depends on it. In today's upheaval within the traditional publishing industry many worthwhile books get rejected out of hand. Major publishers are looking toward known names and relatively certain profits. Conversely, an independent writer can self publish whatever material he wants—junk if he so chooses. The problem comes down to the ease of publishing making it seem less important for a poor writer to improve himself or learn the techniques of writing. That is unfortunate because it has contributed to indie books in general getting bad press. Yet there are thousands of exceptional indie books. The remedy and the challenge for this situation will be to weed out the hacks. Their books will barely sell, especially when reviews give them low ratings. Don't be tempted to join them. In the indie game it's difficult enough to sell books. Give yourself an even chance and learn the craft. Write the best books you can.

POINT OF VIEW: Let's qualify point of view (POV) since it is a subject on which many new writers may not be clear. The POVs used are First person, Second person and Third person.

First Person: This is the subjective "I" and uses I, me, we, us, our—the story is told from the viewpoint of one person. The reader can only know what the narrator knows and the narrator can only know what he experiences or what someone tells him.

Even in first person, which should be clear cut and consistent, writers can make POV mistakes. Assume Roger is telling the story. Roger says, "Homer and I were waiting on the bridge. Suddenly Homer turned and looked toward someone heading our way." Roger just told us what Homer did. He turned his body or maybe his head, he moved his eyes.

But if Roger says, "Homer and I were waiting on the bridge. Suddenly Roger turned and saw someone heading our way." Point of view just changed. Roger got in Homer's head. Roger can't know what Homer saw. He could see Homer turn, but he doesn't know if Homer saw the person or not. Homer may have been looking at a hawk in the sky. Roger would only know what Homer saw if Homer told him.

The most common mistake we see in first person viewpoint books is when the narrator says something like, "The guy was arrogant, irritating me immediately. I could see that Joe thought so, too." No – he couldn't see that at all. He doesn't know what Joe is thinking. He might see a slight frown on Joe's face but he only assumes that Joe thinks the guy is arrogant. Joe might think he has a terrible hair cut.

If the narrator had said "Joe appeared to think so, too," he would have stayed in his own viewpoint and the reader would be aware that Joe might think that.

Careless or inconsistent viewpoint throws the reader off. Sometimes she has to read a sentence twice to decipher it. Or she might accept the narrator's opinion and then later in the book be confused when Joe is supportive of the man that the narrator finds arrogant. These types of mistakes with viewpoint have an impact on the story that then affects the reader. They may seem minor but if they distort the storyline and cause the reader to flounder they undermine the story. Writers using first person must be diligent in keeping the viewpoint character subjective, seeing only from his own eyes, thinking his own thoughts.

This is limiting for the writer. But it is the viewpoint in which most detective and crime thrillers are written. When mastered it is a POV that lets the writer move the story along rapidly. It is up close and personal; it establishes a rapport between the narrative character and the reader. As writer Sol Stein says, "It's an eyewitness account, highly subjective and highly credible." For these reasons, writers of crime thrillers and detective novels favor the first person point of view.

A word of caution: be very careful not to give information to the reader that the protagonist doesn't or couldn't know. In that instance the author's voice leaps off the page and the reader will feel as if she's just been slapped. The least the reader will feel is that the author just made a mistake. And that's not favorable to a writer. Too many of those and she may never read another of your books. She might not even finish the one she has in her hands and that's especially detrimental. She won't be telling her friends about the good book she just read. Worse, she may tell her friends about the terrible book she couldn't even finish. Word of mouth is a writer's best or worst friend. Frequently remind yourself of that.

There is, however, a way around this problem. Some writers use the first person viewpoint for most of the book but in a few chapters move over to third person. This gives them freedom then to introduce scenes that do not include the first person protagonist. John Grisham used this tool effectively in The Racketeer. Grisham, however, wrote in third person viewpoint in his early works. A beginning writer could be expected to do better using third person until he becomes more proficient as his new trade.

Second Person: This viewpoint uses You, the writer speaking directly to the reader. It is rarely used.

Third Person: There are two "versions" here, Third Person Limited and Third Person Omniscient. The omniscient viewpoint is more or less God's viewpoint. The writer can show anything that any character is thinking and can describe any events from the past or any future events that may occur. This is an old fashioned style of writing. Out of favor for quite some time, it is rarely used today. It was popular with early authors such as Joseph Conrad, Jane Austen and other eighteenth and nineteenth century writers.

Third Person Limited is sometimes called the Narrative Mode or often just called Third Person. This is the most common viewpoint in which stories are told. First person is quite popular but third is the most frequently used. At any given time books on store shelves, in racks or being promoted on Internet stores are mainly told in the third person.

In this viewpoint a narrator tells the story in the third person. The pronouns used in this mode are he, she, it, they, them. The actions reported are told and interpreted by one person. Unless one is an experienced writer, it is best if the viewpoint stays with just the narrator. As one becomes more experienced in handling the craft of fiction writing, he can change the POV person, but it is best to do that in a separate chapter. Combining viewpoints in the same chapter can become confusing and as we've already discussed, the last thing you want to do is confuse your reader.

There is a limitation that occurs in Third Person the same as in First Person – the narrator cannot know what is in another person's mind. He cannot assume or say things like, "I watched her stare at her shoes as she considered how to dump her obnoxious boy friend." The narrator may have been talking to her previously about her boy friend, but he can't know what she is thinking as she stares at her shoes. Maybe she thinks she is due for a new pair of sneakers. Be very alert to these types of mistakes. That includes emotions, too. It is easy to assign emotion to a character by the expression on his face. Remember that the narrator must be told what other characters are thinking or feeling or what those characters know. As said earlier, these literary *faux pas* seem small but they add up. Readers don't like the way inconsistencies feel.

GESTURES: It is best to keep your characters' movements and gestures to a minimum. Let the dialogue make the point, not bodily or facial gestures. A few will suffice; be alert to overuse of gestures. Repeating them becomes annoying to the reader.

SPEECHES: Don't let one character ramble on too long. Break up conversation between characters. Your readers don't enjoy speeches any more than you do when you are expecting a friendly exchange. I knew a person once who ended every sentence with "and. . ." She'd take a quick breath and you knew there was going to be no room for you to participate in this conversation.

It was tedious to say the least. Don't let your characters do it.

GRAMMAR is a subject for another book, though it does need to be stressed that a writer should know at least the basic rules of sentence structure, punctuation and spelling. If one is confused as to a rule or choice (effect vs. affect) go to Google. Google knows everything and you can resolve many confusing issues there.

Brian A. Klem, online editor for *Writer's Digest*, tackles the Who/Whom issue and demonstrating with two sentences he goes into subject of a verb, object of a preposition, objective pronoun, and more. Briefly, though, he writes:

It was Carl who broke all the pencils in the house.

You asked whom to the dance?

But instead of memorizing all the rules, Brian comes up with a little trick he says he learned in elementary school: If it can be replaced with "he," you use *who*; if "him" fits better, use *whom*.

He says sometimes you have to split the sentence to see it and gives these examples: *It was Carl—he broke all the pencils in the house. Who* should be used here. *You asked him to the dance? Whom* is the correct choice.

But then Editor Brian says, with tongue in cheek, "When in doubt on the 'who whom' debacle, recast the sentence to avoid the issue altogether."

Good advice, I'd say.

Editor Brian takes on one other pair of easily confused words and their usage:

Which vs. That and has invited me to use his examples.

Here's his rule of thumb:

If the sentence doesn't need the clause that the word in question is connecting, use *which.* If it does, use *that.*

Our office, which has two lunchrooms, is located in Cincinnati.

Our office that has two lunchrooms is located in Cincinnati.

"These sentences are not the same," Brian says. "The first sentence tells us that you have just one office, and it's located in Cincinnati. The clause *which has two lunchrooms* gives us additional information, but it doesn't change the meaning of the sentence. Remove the clause and the location of our one office would still be clear. *Our office is located in Cincinnati.*

"The second sentence suggests that we have multiple offices, but *the office with two lunchrooms* is located in Cincinnati. The phrase *that has two lunchrooms* is known as a restrictive clause because another part of the sentence (*our office*) depends on it. You can't remove that clause without changing the meaning of the sentence."

Brian concludes with "If the information is essential, use *that*. If it's just additional information that's useful but unnecessary, use *which*.

Let's end this little discussion of grammar with a few commonly misused words:

Affect: Influence. Usually a verb.

Effect: A result. Usually a noun.

Except: Excluding. Usually a preposition. Or a verb meaning "to exclude."

Accept: To receive. She accepted the package.

Emigrate: To leave one country to settle in another.

Immigrate: To arrive in a country to live there.

Here's a clever tip:

Emigrate starts with E. Exit. Exit a country.

Immigrate starts with an I. In. Come in a country.

☙⊙℘℞℘⊙❧

■~~~Twelve~~~■

How to Deal With Writer's Block

Writer's Block: A condition believed to exist which freezes an author's ability to create, to produce new work or to continue partially completed work. It is reputed to be either minor or serious and can be so damaging as to destroy a career, preventing an author from ever writing again.

How a writer contracts this condition is seemingly a mystery and no medication has been discovered in research labs to cure it.

What's a writer to do, then?

Dozens of ideas have been put forth as to how one overcomes Writer's Block. They are all put forth by people who believe the block exists in the first place. Many writers contend that there is no such thing. A difference of opinion exists and discussions have been held ad infinitum on the subject. Too often being "blocked" is little more than being lazy, so for openers examine your so-called-block and ask yourself honestly: what is your reason for not writing? If you just don't want to invest the energy, you'll recognize it and that alone may help crumble the block and send you sheepishly back to your desk.

If you are dealing with some major problem in your life or your family life, it is undoubtedly compromising your writing. Of course you must take the steps toward resolving such issues. Perhaps while working at those resolutions you may also be capable of setting them aside for short periods of time while you write.

Substance abuse is not conducive to good writing. Deal with such issues for your own health and for your writing future. Get professional help if needed.

Are you exhausted while trying to write? Perhaps instead of trying to write after a full working day you may want to get up early and write for an hour or so before your work day begins.

Absent any of those intrusions, let's confront the problem head on. Writer's block, like artist's or musician's blocks, basically stems from fear. Fear, or belief that one is unable to produce up to his own expectations or other people's expectations. Once a person starts buying into this fear, that is, accepting or believing it, the fear is given power. Biological power and emotional power.

You may already be aware that our belief systems are so strong and have such a huge effect on us that they can plunge us into illness. There is a considerable amount of data and research on this subject. It has been shown in the laboratory as well as by empirical studies. Even some salesmen, Tony Robbins comes to mind, have made impressive changes in people's lives through helping them change their belief systems. This has also been true of deep belief in religion or prayer. Beliefs can go far in healing us and in keeping us well. What does this have to do with writer's block? A great deal as a matter of fact.

The first thing you can do for your mental writing health is to refuse to compare yourself with other writers. You are not them and they are not you. You are your own unique writer self and the more you write the more that truth is going to surface.

Do not set unreasonable goals for yourself. Perhaps eventually it will make sense for you to write eight hours a day. As a beginning writer it does not. Nor should you set a goal of writing, rewriting, editing, polishing and publishing a novel in the next six months. Don't do that to yourself. By indulging in these types of pressures you can set yourself up for illness and certainly for "writer's block." You may begin to get nervous over your unreasonable goals, fear you can't accomplish them, fear what your family and friends will say if you don't reach goals you've stated. Or, worse, you might decide you don't have what it takes after all.

Do not set yourself up for fear or failure. Follow the suggestions earlier in this book, set a reasonable number of words to produce each day, study writing techniques, read for pleasure, take a walk, relax.

If you do come up against a blank mind, do not give it a label. Don't tell anyone, or yourself either, that you have Writer's Block, as if you just contacted bubonic plague. There are many things you can do to get your juices flowing again. Google will find endless suggestions for you if you want to try them, most of them from authors who believe in the big W.B. demon. The first and most popular advice you'll find is to take a break from your work. Personally, I'd say that's the worst thing you can do. Maybe leave the computer for the evening, take your spouse or significant other to a movie, stop for pie and chocolate on the way home and get a good night's sleep. Or whatever else you had in mind.

Next day at your usual writing time, if you find you are still stumped, blocked, or frozen look around the room and choose some item—the clock on the table, a painting, the wall map above your computer desk—and write a stream of consciousness about it. Just free flow about whatever you have chosen and let it take you wherever it takes you even if it doesn't make sense or if it takes you on an entirely new road. This alone may move you along. Or choose a novel by a writer you like, open to any page and rewrite what that author wrote. Work at it awhile; see if you can improve it. Make it funny or silly. Doing these types of exercises are often quite rewarding. They can be repeated several times though it may not take more than a few before you are bored with it and want to get back to your manuscript.

If you have another piece you are working on it is always a very good idea when you feel "blocked" on your main novel, to go to the other work and spend some time writing there. Or even start a new piece, maybe an article for one of the online magazines such as Ezine.

If your novel still doesn't want to move along, write it anyway. Move down a few spaces so you can find your "blocked" starting place later, and go on with the story. It doesn't matter how rough it is, how bad the writing is or where the story seems to be going, just write. Maybe at that session, or the next one or the one after that, your Muse will suddenly appear and you will find your stride again.

Even if you feel you are writing a lousy book, write it anyway. It may go somewhere in spite of you and probably will. You won't always be at your writing best. Some days you'll write when you feel at your worst. Keep writing. You'll find your best days again and when you reach 'The End' you'll likely discover that you do in fact actually have a book. Your next session at the computer will be to start the rewrite. That's when your book will start to come to life. Don't be too surprised, either, if your Muse shows up through a great deal of the rewriting. That's when mine is at her absolute bossiest.

You are a writer. Refuse to be lazy. Write through your blocks, your easy times and hard times. You will be proud of yourself when you do.

💻~~~Thirteen~~~💻

REWRITING AND PUBLISHING

REWRITING

Michael Crichton had it right: Good books are not written, they're rewritten. If you have finished that sucky first draft we talked about earlier, cheers for you. You have accomplished a truly major undertaking. Few people who are not writers will understand what it took for you to complete that monumental task. But your fellow writers know. We applaud you.

Your project was work, difficult and sometimes seemingly insurmountable work. The good news is that now the fun starts. You are going to enjoy rewriting. Whether you do one draft or ten, your book will get better and better with each rewrite. New ideas will occur to you and your story is likely to change and grow, not necessarily longer but better. You'll find the weak spots and be thrilled by the strong ones, and you will know which is which.

You might not like to hear this suggestion, but it would be good for you to put your manuscript away for a couple weeks and don't peek at it. Let it rest and let your mind rest. You need to get outside of the story that is still bouncing around in your mind. You can do other things during the break, such as thinking about the perfect cover and a killer title and even taking a short rest from the computer if you feel the need

Not everyone chooses to do this. Many prefer to get right back to the novel and start the rewrite at their next sitting. Choose whatever works for you. When you are ready to work on it, save your manuscript file as Rewrite One and begin to read it. Some writers like to print each chapter, read and start hand marking the pages, then keyboarding that chapter into the Rewrite One file. I like to do that on my first rewrite and work on subsequent ones on the computer. Try different approaches and choose the one that is the best fit for you.

Work slowly and carefully during this process. Rewrite sentences. Rewrite paragraphs. Rewrite chapters. Trash-can those parts that do not measure up. It hurts to kill your darlings, as writers say, but if it improves the story, do it. Author Lawrence Block says "I doubt if there is one page in a thousand, throughout the whole of literature, that wouldn't have been improved by the author re-doing it." That might be an exaggeration but he does make the point.

Pay attention to punctuation, misspellings, sentence structure, word choices and formatting. Write new sections where needed. Do you have pet words you tend to use too often? Search for them with the Find function in your word processing program. When you have finished the chapter, go back to the first sentence and read the chapter straight through. Does it progress sensibly? Are there weak spots? Did it end with a question or a "knock on the door" to make you want to turn the page? If you are satisfied with it, read it aloud. This is often a surprise. Your ears may catch things that your eyes didn't. Writers now have the option of having their computers read their printed words back to them. Either way, it is good advice for every chapter.

Take the same steps with the next chapter and each succeeding one. When you reach the end you should feel that it is either finished or that it needs another draft.

When you decide it is as good as it can be, take the next major step: read the manuscript from beginning to end. By the time you get to the last page you may have made a few more changes, many more changes or none at all.

At this point you may indeed be finished. If you had been working with a quality critique group throughout the writing of the novel, you could ask or hire one of them to read the manuscript. He or she may catch errors you missed. If you're not affiliated with a critique group it is probably time for you to turn your work over to an editor. If you don't know of any or how to find a good one (there are scammers in the industry, do be careful) join a good online writing group where information is shared. Some excellent ones on Facebook at this time are: Novel Publicity Network, World Literary Café, Authors and Book Lovers and Indie Writers Unite. Type the name into Facebook's search window and join the groups.

When you have completed all of the above and polished your manuscript to the best it can be, you are ready for the next step and it is a big one.

PUBLISHING

This is not a book about publishing but as a new writer you will surely want to know what your options are. There are basically three avenues you can pursue: Traditional publishers like The Big Six, smaller presses or independent self-publishing.

The Big Six refers to New York's largest traditional book publishers. There are steps to take in order to pursue traditional publishing. It has been many years since a writer could approach a publishing house and expect a favorable response. Writers need an agent. Your first action should be to learn how to write a query letter that will catch an agent's attention. You have at most a paragraph to do that and for some uber busy agents perhaps only a sentence. Along with your query you also need to include a synopsis and a chapter or more, whatever the agent specifies in his or her submissions guidelines.

It is important to write a quality query letter as well as a synopsis that includes the ending. Google knows everything so it will be your best friend through learning the procedure for publishing. You could Google "Query" or "How to Write a Query Letter." You might also want to go to a blog that is of immense help to many writers, one written by former literary agent Nathan Bransford. Find him easily via Google. You will discover considerable information on writing and publishing as well as data on agents.

In addition to the Big Six there are smaller presses to pursue. And these days there is also self or independent publishing.

A great many writers, even traditionally published authors, have moved to independent publishing. Ask Google to search for eBook publishers. There are dozens of such publishers already in business and many more entering the marketplace every week. Unless your book really is junk, you should not have a problem finding an eBook publisher. That may change in the future as the successful ePublishers become more and more selective as to what they will accept. However, if you had the book professionally edited, it most likely is not junk at all and you should succeed in getting your book published. You do not need an agent to submit to an ePublisher.

There is much more to know about publishing and certainly about marketing, promoting your books and social networking. Independent authors are turning the publishing world upside down. This is only the beginning. Big changes are afoot in the months and years ahead. Get on board now. The more you learn and understand, the better equipped you will be and the better your chances to become a best-selling author.

Welcome to the wonderful, exciting, rewarding world of fiction writing.

✓~~~The Last Word~~~✓

A personal note to my readers

Thank you so much for buying and reading this book. I hope it helps you in every way you want it to. You are welcome to contact me with any comments, questions or suggestions, in fact that would please me greatly. If this book does serve you and if you have completed your novel, I would be thrilled to hear that from you.

I wish you the very best as you discover the joy, and sometimes frustration, of fiction writing.

Warmest regards,

Karleene Morrow

Email: KarleeneMorrow@gmail.com
Website: http://www.karleenemorrow.com

❧⋘⋙❧

16017653R00073

Made in the USA
Charleston, SC
01 December 2012